CW01335745

Seasons

By the Same Author

Journey to Mount Tamalpais, Second Edition, Litmus Press, 2021

Shifting the Silence, Nightboat Books, 2020

Time, Nightboat Books, 2019

Surge, Nightboat Books, 2018

Night, Nightboat Books, 2016

Life is a Weaving, Galerie Lelong, 2016

Premonition, Kelsey Street Press, 2014

Sea & Fog, Nightboat Books, 2012

Master of the Eclipse, Interlink Books, 2009

In the Heart of the Heart of Another Country, City Lights Books, 2005

Seasons, The Post-Apollo Press, 2005

In/somnia, The Post-Apollo Press, 2002

There, The Post-Apollo Press, 1997

Of Cities & Women (Letters to Fawwaz), The Post-Apollo Press, 1993

Paris, When It's Naked, The Post-Apollo Press, 1993

The Spring Flowers Own & The Manifestations of the Voyage,
    The Post-Apollo Press, 1990

The Arab Apocalypse, The Post-Apollo Press, 1989

Journey to Mount Tamalpais, The Post-Apollo Press, 1986

The Indian Never Had a Horse & Other Poems, The Post-Apollo Press, 1985

Sitt Marie-Rose, The Post-Apollo Press, 1982

From A to Z, The Post-Apollo Press, 1982

Five Senses for One Death, The Smith, New York 1971

Moonshots, Beirut 1966

ETEL ADNAN

Seasons

THE POST–APOLLO PRESS / LITMUS PRESS

Seasons © Etel Adnan, 2008
Second Printing, 2022

All rights reserved.

ISBN: 978-0-942996-66-1

Cover drawing by Etel Adnan
Book design by Simone Fattal
Typesetting by Kathleen Wilkinson
   in Minion for the text and Arno Pro Display for the titling

The Post-Apollo Press was founded by Simone Fattal in 1982. It is now managed by Litmus Press and distributed by Small Press Distribution in Berkeley, CA. *Seasons* is a Post-Apollo Press reprint published by Litmus Press.

Litmus Press publications are made possible by the New York State Council on the Arts with support from Governor Kathy Hochul and the New York State Legislature. Additional support for Litmus Press comes from the Leslie Scalapino – O Books Fund, The Post-Apollo Press, individual members and donors. All contributions are fully tax-deductible.

Cataloging-in-Publication Data is available from the Library of Congress.

Litmus Press
925 Bergen Street, Suite 405
Brooklyn, New York 11238
litmuspress.org

Distributed by Small Press Distribution
1341 Seventh Street
Berkeley, California 94710
spdbooks.org

Seasons

ACKNOWLEDGEMENT

Section 1 was published in *New,*
Issue 3, 2007, Paris, under the title "A Season."

for Joanne Kyger

1

There are imperceptible writings. Language's triangular shape is applied to vision: a rush of Being. Pressure is applied on time, bending it. The curvature is imparted to one's soul trying to escape from the abyss while dreading to fall even lower. Greece comes to the rescue. Doors are sliding and preventing the future's return.

This morning a woman disappeared in the sun's obliquity. Much later the moon appeared. There's regularity to the presence of things, the numinous flowering of this spring, but uncertainty about the lack of will in this piece of wood. A deer, facing a car's headlights, is a reminder of existence.

Being is invisible to all the senses, why are the senses then excluded from the promise of thinking? Or are they? Is adhering to one's skin life's sole purpose? Undulating movements pit themselves against the body's bewildered surface, there, where death is structural. When the drought reaches the valley, stories replace the river.

As Earth doesn't expand, power does, and may get out of hand. By consuming itself it will consume this turbulent planet, including its volcanoes. Does one leave in one's room a shape emptied of its body? Its mind? Is mind more ubiquitous than flesh? If so, they're not homogenous, but alien to each other, though interdependent. Is reality to be trusted? There are gaps into which we either fall to die or to start living.

In a season of migration movies are preferred to books. Luminosity is a different language, the result of a confluence of methods used by Nature. A reel played backwards, that's the future. Wherever one looks one finds that space is filled with the past along with steep cliffs, big fires. Although the moon escaped the disaster, the future will not. Poisons connect with their destination in beautiful plants. A lawyer loses his argument. The voyage is delayed.

Bodies are born from bodies. It's more dangerous to disbelieve one's senses than keep God on the back burner. There's moss on the windowsill, even in warm weather. The erasure of one facet of the mind and the emergence of the next could concern the pleasure to kill. Love is flood. Flash! Zeus, enamored, tumbling through Space.

Ancient rivers drift into ancient memories. They create watery fields the way music transforms breathing air into a subject of contemplation for the ears. Flat lands. One drop of water added to another can make an angel appear. The moon tears apart the illuminated clouds and reigns alone.

O the Syrian desert mounted by its young emperors in the steel days of Rome! Its salt has melted in the Euphrates. Further north the spring has planted miles of orchards. Frantic flowers whisper to the wind. Birds use corridors of air within the air for their flight. Their shadows come from the soul. It is necessary not to stay still; the voyage is family.

I want to walk in mountainous countries. Some nations are

sitting and crying in front of screens larger than their borders. Their brains are starting to fall apart. I listen. Of course, all this is perceived as silence, in the midst of storms, under heaven's explosion.

History doesn't drive on camels anymore but it's still eating dust. Communication lines, since, are buried deep under the skin. Fog is pouring over history, and not lifting. Disorder is chronic, surrender, erotic by essence. Victims are dangerous in their revenge.

Can one break memory the way one breaks stone with stone? Is memory's function to first break down, by its own means, then pick up the pieces and reassemble them, but clumsily, never in the way they used to be? Is a fractured mind just fractured, or is it multiplied? Would a brain, collapsed but re-sewn, enjoy again the spring of California's northern frontier and know that only music can ever represent the penetration of one's eyes by flowering trees?

… As if pain were a metaphor for pleasure. Saying this, the book is closed. To run water in gutters and feed the blue jays on berries is Nature's perfect balancing act. It would be preposterous to use theories for climbing California's rust-colored mountains. Love is not a game for lovers. Going through destruction, bodies break either like glass or soft cake.

Shiny red peppers! Green peppers! Women walk between tomatoes and leeks, in a season of war; that's not unusual. It's rather like swimming in the summer. Things move fast in a world of silence and disruption. In the morning, pushing dreams aside, it's good to take a walk down alleys of linden trees, vegetable gardens.

Fish are jumping when a heat wave sails through a bleak luminescence. Sounds made by passersby. (Lorca fell to bullets.) The ocean, beyond the hills, embodies a unilateral decision made by geography, its intensity alleviated by its beauty. Active principles keep Earth rolling on schedule. The center will remain central.

Clouds are war's first casualties. Laurels are spread on beds where lovers will spend their nights. It's a time when the description of paradise leads the mind to insurrection, chaos. The sky looms big in shallow pools on broken streets. A four-year-old Iraqi boy has been amputated of his two arms after an American air raid blew up his quarter. When he woke up he asked: "when will I get them back?"

The oak tree is growing with anxiety and the olive tree with the anticipation of rain. The mountain behind is listening to thunder. Mind and weather fuse, in the mind's owner and in the weather. The land is obsessed with rivers, floods and heat. Memory is helpless: mind cannot control it.

No object can compete with a sound's intimacy. Anarchy, in our veins, creates fever, confusion, though we remember that owls don't bark. One wave, one hour at a time. Then wind blows on sheets of air, raising spray and foam. A gale blinds the view.

A treacherous span of water disrupts the traffic. "Detour" says the road. In stormy seasons, time stretches, reaches over to transcendence. Fish swim uninterruptedly. Mountain lions hunt, with an anger that makes them thirsty, thirsting for air.

Cinema impresses the impressionable. A customer comes for what he knows not to be there: this is called seeking illusions. Through tunnels, matter, jealously, follows images. Being is the fourth dimension, and mind, too. Therefore Being equals mind and vice-versa. What about the other dimensions? Non-Being is the invincible force that pushes Being up the hill. The same with sorrow. A film in its entirety forms a single image. As oceanic as longing.

Writing: the body's imprint on wet sand. Spring is element of thinking; perfect tool. Poetry is a question of speed and time, speed and time. For insomniacs, mind – while all other things are excluded – plays games with itself. Then language, in those nights, reveals itself as being our essential self. In dreams, we fly as fast as we think, and we're rather happy.

Time passes from right to left. Planets intrude on the sky. A rain of daffodils appeases the drought. A ghost moves from room to room, keeps hearts pounding. Any noise slides on walls the way light transports itself from its source to this environment. A woman goes to the cliff, and waits, standing, and non-visibility envelops her totally.

In solitude let things be predictable. A walk through the forest brings out sounds, scents and visions of fern. The encounter creates desire. The deer are running down, bringing along their offspring. In the night trees look taller, the redwoods in particular. This forest is another continent.

And what do the police say when they realize that suicidal women could be beautiful? (they eat fish and chips). They notice that the century's first half is the whole cut in two. With a knife.

Circling an event on paper. In streets. At oblivion's center. Breaking the circle brings terror, as the radio announces. Shut the radio! Let light come from the other hemisphere. This garden's circumference is inconsequential. It doesn't threaten travelers. We need to find out where the body was lying, in that absence, that distance. In comes wilderness, i.e. the heart's, in these days, these latitudes.

She destroyed the spring to be had. Description of the loss: bottles lined up, with leftover wine in them. Sometimes, sweet poison. An eye for an eye. Love's impossibility multiplied by mirrors. A woman bartender. Everything waiting for a non-event. News about the weather posted from early in the morning. There was nothing else to fill the brain with. The current did pass, but was diverted at twilight. The flight of a fly was heard. That was all. It recurred.

A season for Dionysus, baby-god born with speech impediment. Owing existence to the Orient. His ancestry born in blood. Every sunset reproduces his birth. Look at the sky! His language: dance in the imperative tense. From the Tragic Times there's nothing left. Someone ate fish in the kitchen. The young god got raped by demented women, his lost virginity echoed by mountains blanketed with snow. Zeus was aging. His grandchild was dying.

When the world and the mind face each other with ultimate intensity, they cancel out. With its electrical system broken down, the body doesn't qualify anymore for a name. One can then water the garden with wine.

Dionysus passed the torch on to Orpheus. On a fatal morning. The sea blackened, split. There are dimensions that we ignore although they emit sounds and they flicker. Invisible equations rain, and birds dread that tempest. The coast is an open shore.

The season is stubborn. During some nights thick with scents and sounds, redwoods bend, speak, waive or express their bewilderment. These magnificent athletes mark their grounds with the performance of unsuspected ceremonies, rites, in their unknown modes of being. The ocean's sound waves are heard on the moon.

Ravaged by darkness, the moon is dangerous. The spring has hit its periphery. Down on earth, savage seas are moving toward their middle under melancholy's heavy banners. Disasters are not acceptable. The hidden is inbuilt in thinking. Nature's daily presentation of diversity distracts one from the nonessential.

Light shows its impatience by creating shadows. We project our longings on the horizon's precarious line, and separate words from the objects they're meant to represent. The moon doesn't speak any of our languages.

To contemplate an empty sky until it gets lit with stars, then ask the imagination to seek other realms of emptiness. Spring mediates love for the sake of wet leaves, bobcats… In stricken areas, it wears its best attire.

Master of velocity, light bores into the tree trunks of these woods. Blue moon over green waters. The beach's impenetrable beauty lends its transparency to the soul in order to institute Being, in a joint creation.

Life concentrates on the mind's surface: it either accelerates time, or discontinues it. The storm is wiping out visibility. Matter skids out of itself. In this annihilation, only the forest survives, and the streams that are running through. Chaos in dormant dwellings.

The Night Palace stands tall by the ocean. We need to explore that reality. Green emergence. The mountain oversees turbulent waters that carry erosion. Tragedies borrow their blood from such places. No ways to reach the top other than on disturbed and crooked roads. Here, one says the hell with the future!

On the mesa they do away with nebulous desires. The sun, as it rises, consumes the foothills as well as the will, leaving a trail of haze. This human race is driving space vehicles into more wilderness: Prometheus of a new kind, not chained but let loose for a doom differed, the voyage being the prize.

An angel falls in the thick of the night to witness war, confusion and pain. He lingers until the late hours for a walk among the planet's rose bushes. He encounters deer jumping fences across hills lost in mist. As far as he can see, whales follow their route to the North. Smooth pebbles lie on the beach.

The sky writes tales on mercurial lines; they mean resonance. A woman plunges in her expectations; her longing is hard to bear. Planes land smoothly; white sails go sailing. Storms are peripatetic creatures of the weather. Open land, open sea. Trains cross reservations and whistle, clouds pick up their pace and follow. Hot streams within the ocean bring to it instability.

In the high season, rains fall horizontally while tamarisk, scattered by dry riverbeds, thrives on the ranch. The area is an undeclared factory of hallucinatory herbs. The spirit blows over a moon drunk with gentian and sage. Matter is indeed a wandering substance. The mind feels a fatal attraction for the impossible; it turns the body into a tool, and a destination.

Nature doesn't do things. It's not available for any kind of trade. Before sinking, the sun deposits a filament of fire on the ocean's edge. A battle is raging. One army's aim is to humiliate the other. Nature, though, will remain relevant: it's Being's outer image, Being's outer Being.

Time is a dramatic performance. Where Lorca fell a cactus grew. Along the road there was a short-lived jubilation. Ecstasy is lightning, and love, apparition, therefore disappearance. When the creek swelled the deer, suddenly, camouflaged their terror. The car survived the crash. The brain didn't.

Be the wind, the folly that floods the fields with wine. Dionysus is blinded by the sun setting in his eyes. Sitting next to him at a table, Cavafy yearns for young men. Wears garlands. He says the air is clear. He writes it down.

Defeat drowns with the defeated, like fish. The ocean is an enormous plantation that produces, instead of rice, sardines, algae… It breathes and gives breath. Its anger beneficially clears the spirit.

Eucalyptus doesn't grow for the shade it provides but for sheer pleasure. Plane trees spend their nights on the county's lower meadows. During the winter their branches burn in the woodstoves. Silence falls gradually. Sleep becomes another form of awareness.

Gold-crown sparrows, finding an air draft, greet their happiness with chirps. They participate in the earth's vigor. By night's fall their energies are dissipated. That's when some people mix wine with beer. They dream of their tribe of origin.

Small towns suit the full moon. In the bars, loud music increases the natural weariness of the customers. The season is undamaged but there's danger in the grass. An apprehension of things to come. That woman doesn't shoot heroin, being naturally high. Fate is cruel and its damage irreparable.

When the storm gathers momentum, the three ravens that are my neighbors fly down from the pine tree and walk in the middle of the street. One is limping. The cold wind shakes everything out of its comfort. It's time to leave, to catch a train.

Women enter their bed with their lover and feel their loneliness. There's mystery to their flesh. On Saturn's moons a watery stuff has been found. This night is not a night although it's not a day.

To think is not to contemplate, it's to witness. We have to deal with the events that happen in the Palace's danger zone… By the dusty alley's end, the ocean unfolds its unlimited space. That cliff is poetry's jumping board. Words are cracked open, reused in bits and pieces. There's much agitation. Spring unattached itself from its elements. It has become Being.

Orbiter 2 is sent to Mars. Human eyes will scan that new space by proxy, with cold instruments. Vivid greens, in the garden, are emerging from the snow, light snow, and sounds are filtering through the door. It's Schubert seeking shelter. The season, in February, is stirring under the ground's skin.

Trees are not extensions of the self but pure phenomena. Their time does not intersect with ours. They travel differently. They are cyclical, and envied for that. Their lives are not part of our tragic continuum; they have a lightness, a closeness to water, air or fire, all of their own.

Accompanied by its train of clouds, the sky enters, and settles in the room. We will share the night. We trust the mountain to remain in one piece while we sleep. In the morning the light will be of the same silver that makes black-and-white photography shine.

The mind travels at the speed of light. Probably faster. The theorem is short. Objects bring out life's infinity. For Being, everything is a phenomenon; therefore it can't think itself. Thoughts are also phenomena in relation to it, and in themselves. They're splendid events. Spring is dangerous, like love. And love survives the lovers.

There are no horses around, unless the sun be one. The eucalyptus is building a hedge for the moon so that the latter would know at which door to knock. Not the Great Wall of China. Ocean hypnotizes. The Aztecs knew two things above all: that human predators would disembark one day and that mind produces light.

The hidden face of the moon and the hidden one of Being… In where is the difference? A room is built to accommodate windows. A deck. Branches. Sleet. Language interferes, separates plants from animals, O original sin! Voices come from the outside and drill channels till the brain. We were meant to create signs, not ideas. Trial balloons. Hot sand and surf.

They blame their failure on the season's precocity, the moon's early rise. The eye and the "I", same sound and probably same thing. That's why, in a single room there are many exits for the soul. We move in order to stop the thinking, let something else take over. In moving there's rest.

Humidity provides rain for the oak trees of the National Park. Their manifest destiny is to be oak trees. They remember those who walk by them. They drink from the ditch. A dismal prison was attacked by a powerful country.

A glass of water on a table. Some yards away, a plum tree. The mountain, still there, watching. The recurrence of the waves is taken for granted. Their sound, too. We marvel at this: that an apple is an apple. All evidence is tragic. It's also inbuilt in seasons.

In crevasses, gullies, troughs, there's youthful energy. Tides transfixed by the clarity of the atmosphere on illuminated mornings. It's suddenly very cold: shells on the beach, driftwood, traces of salt in the foam.

Cameras register atmospheric events such as the rustling of the forest, the drizzle, the fog. During the night of the equinox the downpour broke the levees. The earth shook everything around. Maps had to be drawn anew.

When spring starts to turn into old wine the air gets to be wet and the mind exuberant. Messages arrive from the forest's edge about the state of the water system. The breeze climbs high on the hills and the war returns to the front page. The ocean remains motionless in the midst of its storms.

The fleet has left for the Indian Ocean. To carry its terror the furthest it can. The crews are on alert.

It's late at night. In a matter of a few hours a motion picture has covered the lives of a bunch of people. In the same lapse of time the air has hardly stirred, the trees have hardly grown and the animals in the surrounding farms have not turned in their sleep. The season is passing by.

2

But these clouds, these fallen leaves, belong to History too, like you and me. Airplanes fly over Paris when the skies are high. Clouds darken when a war looms over the horizon. Winds brought melancholy in their wake and some rain, some warning. Rain! barely falling and still enough for sadness to settle where pain had left. Then, a blizzard falling on two lovers.

Fragility of the season, of life. Ephemeral lodging. Roots are left uncovered, drying, or perhaps already rotting on the soil's soft surface. Is anyone aware of the sun dimming, bearing a civilization into obscurity? In the East, some rays sometimes escape.

Heartbeats are borrowed from the sun's pulse; along the riverbank some objects, impregnated with our thinking, soar. We are not condemned to our fate. Nobody can prevent the trees from breaking or succeed in erasing a season sheltered by our will.

We can't blame autumn leaves for the morning's late rise, nor the person we loved for the fog that filled her eyes when both the season and the mind feared her inevitable downfall. A shiver lingers in my limbs in spite of an absence longer than what time allows. Where do intimate things hide? could it be in the mass of flesh, bones, ligaments, disposables that run to rivers… We project them in magnificent drawings by Rembrandt, in Mozart's melodies, although they can well rejoin that cancer that ate Hiroshima. We caress with our spirit the withdrawn manifestations of the unknown.

Sinuous lines within their bark pull the linden trees upward. They sing. There are other trees in the forest: birch, elm, ginkgo, firs, the oak is native (so is the sunrise). Trees witness our interferences, they don't choose what to see. They look straight ahead into a labyrinth where the temperatures descend Duchamp's staircase down to where gold ceases to be a metal. Short animals run for cover.

To change continents. Poets used to walk across countries; they now sit motionless. There were no mountains, over there, on the horizon's hidden side. Flat lands beget flat ideas. Same for commerce. There's nothing to exchange, anatomy being the only thing we bargain for. The boats were strong on the transcontinental river that was swelling in large, symphonic waves. Silver was generously used after the Aztecs were slaughtered. Yes, days get shorter over disappearing empires. There's a season now that we enter with broken illusions, gloves and sweaters. The woman walking toward the ocean is slowing down her pace.

Nothingness, unknown to the universe, concerns only the mind, that supposedly all-knowing, immaterial, unfathomable non-spatial location that could be an ethereal substance visiting the body. The body responds without asking the mind's permission, and often outside its attention. The whole system named the "I" is unreliable, unbalanced. When it goes astray it carries with it all the seasons. Certainty has no boundaries, therefore no foundation. It's a dangerous growth. Outside one's head, non measurable spaces. Imagination is the mind's visitor, the one most needed to pilot the pitiful body that follows.

Today, it looks as if we're doomed. The sky is bent on itself. Gaza

Street is flooded with blood. Nature is howling. The wind is transgressing the mind's primary function of securing permanence. Space is the body's prime desire. Stars ignore what it means to worry. Sheets of grayness dampen the spirit.

In a savage season a displaced light means revolution. Here's an object with no name: it's not a melon, not a screwdriver. Spirit wanders with the season, becomes sea. Projected to the wind by the wind. Existing is surfacing: a granite block surging from Lake Tenaya or life from sperm. From solid ground or from the invisible itself everything is emergence. Autumn is not summer transformed.

A watch: time's favorite trunk, shipped to India, to Moon or Mars… Does time escape when a hunter steps on it? When illumination comes to the heart love lusts for air. That woman used to close her door, with regularity, lit by her will to stay alive. A rancher is preoccupied by the rainy season. Each bull a Minotaur.

Through the cataclysmic innocence of the sky light is bringing down its intensity. Forest fires spread on screens, our eyes not burning. A rabbit is running through flames, the image is shifting to something else. There's a crowd out there followed by the unfolding of a mountain range. A night of surrender. Patches of asphalt inhabit the inner vision the way bacteria swim in blood vessels. The path is as lonely as the traveler who takes it.

Estranged, disoriented is the moon in its extraterritorial landscape. Born to be moving, dying. Clouds stir the waters the way passion stirs gray eyes into luminosity. There's a need for this flow. Some spirits never connect with the bodies assigned to them. They turn into angels. The river flows fatally; it's nothing but itself, therefore it's you and I.

Why doesn't the sun ever skip a day? Having watched the rain, writers lie their lives on paper. Peasants bend on fields of artichokes, lettuce, corn. Here comes the ocean. The woman walks toward it. From the top of the pyramid of Chichén Itzá the sky is a perfect dome. We're enclosed on sacred grounds. Here the jungle grows according to divine measurements. Our civilization's growth is cancerous.

A musical score, a no-man's-land, that's the season. A crow flies over the Garden's plane trees, the green ones turning red. Indians of the Americas are descending from their mountains holding torches. Valleys are yellowing between granite and residual thoughts. Neither a season of justice nor of oblivion. History's routine. Whose defeat, whose victory? No certitude, only some strange traces.

So where are we? Counting leaves, blades of grass, pebbles, snails, is better than counting words. It's a matter of murdering abstractions. The formulation of new propositions deletes innocence. Adverbs are protesting? Let them wait for the winter.

Once upon a time the sea was luminous, and hungry. As smooth as a young girl's legs. From there it was pure Being. The moment has come for acknowledging that something has to be done for keeping the inner vision inside.

When a bird is hit by a hunter the shot raises the animal by a few inches, then brings it down. Stop the car and cry. Sawdust. Cottonous spaces. To anticipate shrubs with barbaric pleasure.

There's an outburst of wind followed by hale. The temperature is descending the scale like a Hollywood star, dismissed with no possible remission.

There's language for every frontier. *Allegro ma non troppo.* Not too far from here waves have a way to enter without giving notice. Night falls like a knife, not to say a guillotine. On the watch, movements are regular, subdued. They beat like a heart. Michael Strogoff is unreachable, not resurrecting, though the pounding of his horse is here, to be heard.

On that August 11, an eclipse. Central event. At the beginning was the eclipse. Reflected in a pool of Mayan milk. Pursuing the perfect circle. Before millennia and not in autumn. The sun is soft, distributing soft patches of bright light between the high clouds.

Light added on light. Silver's luminosity. Who is granting us such a well-being? To soar through Space and return, oh just once! There's infinity over there. It's a question of grace. Desire's pure energy can cover oceans. That's where it thrives, in hurricanes or stilled tropical seas, in day and night, in chaos. Happily.

Refreshingly. Cold but not icy waters are flowing on mountain sides. The remaining gods are incapable of any decision. We don't need them. The sun is enough.

  Would the forest lose its birds the way an immigrant leaves behind the child he has been? Wolves and foxes get along together when the land is depleted. The sunrise, this morning, was uncluttered, like the sound of Miles Davis' trumpet. In the background, the ocean's inevitability. O the sun's fury when the bull keeps racing over the matador's dead body! Hills surround the stands. A high plateau raises the scene. Life is boiling. One's spirit covers all the space there is.

  Rivers carry dead heroes to larger waters. Were they caught watching birds' flights on the glass panels of their palaces, and how were they able to fight if their nights were peopled with their own dead ancestors? Days are getting shorter; what if one day they decide not to move?

  Nature asks the same questions that children do: where were they before they were born? Why can't they take their growing tree to school with them? Where's the sun coming from? Last night it was warmer than expected and beyond the small towns it was all silence. Icebergs are melting and sounds emerging from their midst. Buzz. Silence again. Thoughts take off and do not return.

To compute the weather is beyond our powers. Skies follow skies, we don't. We're satisfied with high ceilings made of high and interlocking branches. Not a garden, she said, a land. The fountain is the heart of this property. Cézanne's apples are tumbling off the tablecloths. On the ground they find a thin line of water digging a narrow trench. It's time to hurry.

This season's borders are erased by the next one's. Where are they? No wonder one takes refuge in rivers, in or near them. Silencing the search, one falls into the most devastating question: if I am this river how does it happen that I walk in one direction while it flows in an other?

News from Copernicus crater: the eclipse is lifting We rush into the Night Palace. A season has in common with childhood that neither one lasts enough. Leaves fall and fall. Those that stayed orange or yellow shine under the rain, or the snow. The light is dimming. A multitude of tiny sounds proliferate. This happens regularly. A slight hallucination. The displacement of a leaf.

The suddenness of an island in one's life. Mountains arrested in dominant varieties of green. Panoramic quality of the soul at sea level, at light's line of origin. Ancient geographies over which Hölderlin's body navigates. Don't let your thoughts interfere with your senses: to move is to open up space.

A touch of blood, like a fine rain, fills the consciousness. Some countries are in a state of permanent war. Field of vision and field of thinking merging, then overlapping. Big waves are bringing bad news. Horses are racing in the land of the two rivers. This autumn's splendor is feeding anguish.

Out of this world, yes, but why and to where? The ocean is behind the trees. A long procession is carrying a dead fly through the forest all the way to a field of luminous olive trees. Non-native plants are not suffering in this environment. Same laws of physics rule the baggage and the traveler. Being transcending itself toward non-Being.

The mind is excited by the tide's return. Larger currents are coming in. A bank of whales. There are sides to one's humanness that have to be discarded. To remember that a body is a mass of minerals irrigated by a system of mineral liquids. Dry wood is going to feed fires.

The universe resembles the mind, appearing to be spherical. Meteoric thoughts and rockets cross it. No stable space, space moving in space. Propulsion of the self outside itself. A chair abandoned to the weather. Heartbeats. If it weren't for the sun the world would have not existed. Oh the steep descent of the season into its effects!

Bitter herbs. Afternoons losing weight, height. Small books unread. Socrates, a midwife under the weather. Wind blowing with fury. Angels standing in row, with their usual patience. No word for what happened down the road. A skeptical attitude is incompatible with reality.

They figured sacred architecture by observing the forest. Windows are fluorescent apertures. Friends still in Mexico. The atmosphere over there is both older and lighter. Rebellious in its silence, – and distance.

  A stiff little rain and a stiff little wind. One's thinking staggering from sentence to sentence. Tired is the world. Scrambled clouds dissolving in black pan. A familiar forest is friendlier during the night. Dreaming of Mediterranean fountains.

  A childhood of thorns and roses. The schoolyard ready for hurt knees. First rains always a surprise. The miracle of wet earth, wet dust. Hoods dripping. Cats running ferociously for shelter. Threatening cars spitting water as they roll, going to do strange things.

  The moon's sedition is contaminating the sky. Intolerant weather. On evenings like this, Nietzsche used to write letters to his mother. The world has no individuality. It's alien, anyway. The mind doesn't take off from material objects but from immateriality. It's in the brain's obscurity that we see light.

The more we go into something, the more it recedes. It's not even a race. Blindness, incapacity, who knows! This mind's structure doesn't make sense.

I saw airplanes land between water and ground. The hour was unsure. Within the ocean, the change of seasons is hard to discern. Sea lions are by now autonomous. Around the Farallones Islands there's carnage. Unnoticed, I stand by the shore, the turbulence.

From inside that same brain, in the dark, luminous thoughts ooze about one's destiny. Our souls are sinking, making muffled sounds, our lives defoliated. Trees losing their names along their leaves. We walk in the lack of a breeze, in the cold.

Trains move at high speeds, blurring vision, large bands of green hanging in the air. What can one do about the eclipse that's already the subject of a book? News gets around of a premature and devastating snowstorm. Tranquility made sinister. Moving by the fence, crossing the street, realizing that suffering is not always feeling pain. Absolute there-ness of a tree.

A few seconds of love create havoc in History. When the mind brings itself to its own awareness we say "I am." Then Nature interferes and it's a moment of revelation. Words follow and innocence is destroyed. The agility of thinking can terrify, it can also … take bicycles for galaxies.

In the concept of Nature we include specific entities: jasper, lemons, you, a bunch of paper… A particular linden tree had occupied my attention for years. The story went beyond the simple, though permanent encounter. The relation was similar to the desire felt for a young man in a Paris street that I saw once for a few seconds. In midstream.

The sky can be for Being a perfect metaphor: it's there, and non-definable. Inhabited, still independent. Being is mind and outside the mind; it tips over into bliss or terror. No coffins for charred plants, burnt flowers, decomposing former fruit-bearing trees, vineyards, all of them prolongations of nervous systems, cemeteries for dreams.

The weather is dry. Like Arabic writing, a bird flies from right to left. People are in dark dresses, for the season is crumbling. At least, a short day. To the naked eye, Jupiter is white, Mercury, pinkish, Mars, butterscotch color. Traffic. Noise.

Black ink between intimations of sunshine. A coat. Shoes. A friendly bonnet. A muffled trombone. A restless blue jay. Spotted grounds. Fermentation. Only the live speak to the live.

Nights are taking over. There's something cinematic to reality. A curtain is slowly drawn. It's beyond language. Some children never mutate. A stranger was lost on the trail; he's possibly dead by now. Lakes. Little elks stick to their parents. When everything is said, it's obvious that deep down it's hard to find a purpose to anything whatsoever.

Return of the cold. The city is keeping the night high and lit. The prostitutes are out early, at street corners. To smile, to follow a client into a warmer room. Not a city in a time of war. Too distracting a place for angels. The ominous location for one's fears is one's self.

Asked if he was free to see, an owl responded that it only sees those who see him. But the road is narrow. Unpaved. Pristine in its commonness. Bordered by eucalyptus. Poison ivy shines through debris of twigs, acorns, pine needles. Certain kinds of weather accommodate our melancholy.

Celestial objects perform their assigned duties. They cover unfathomable distances as a matter of course. We all are moving, but from where to where? The owl has no answer. It's waiting for the moon to appear.

No stars in the night. A sky of black ashes with no directions. Down on the plain houses are scattered, windows closed, panes drawn in. There's water over there close to a cluster of chestnut trees. In daytime their shadows are immense. Some strange element takes sometimes hold of them, puts them in a frantic state.

Cabin, fireplace, epiphany. Lions on TV, thirsty in a faraway land. A sweeping landscape. Then a deconstructed image of a van. Above, it's not heaven but hell. In the sun's vicinity. This road doesn't lead to a cabin. It keeps going.

In the meantime, autumn displaced itself to the mountains, dragging along Delphi's temples. The rocks are angry. Traces of divinities among them. A world asking to be abandoned to itself. On the other side, an older sanctuary still half buried: Sikyonou, whose honorary citizen I have been made. At last, a home.

In Yosemite Valley the body felt weightless. All the way to the Merced River's beginning. No past or future there. Only to eat, drink and touch granite. There, awareness detaches itself from thinking. The mind becomes a sense added to the other senses. No concepts; just a total, uncluttered way of being.

At the confluence of spirit and matter, or mind and environment, there's a continuous spark. Pulled down by the afternoon's implacable passing, there's no way to see the beach. I carry years of wandering on my back. Would like to shed them.

What is this thing called love? Although too old to be of any interest, the question faces us many times a day. It has a special sound to it, ties with many other things. A mountain looms whenever an answer appears. Let's turn the question around. Does the mountain worry if we love it or not? Does our looking at it transform it? I guess it does.

And then, there's the moon. Her existence poses this crucial interrogation: does Being hide permanently a hidden face, the way she does? The sky is vast beyond any possibility to imagine its expanse. Thus, the solar system is relatively intimate.

This river rushing down from its mountainous pass is offering a new realm, a new language to be learned. A new brain may be needed, and some more time. Forests keep secret rivers, large ones, and at their borders oversized suns are eating up the world.

The fireplace is fed pinewood and glasses are filled with wine. Concepts are disappearing at the rhythm of animal species. Let's have a celebration! Foot soldiers are running for an onslaught. Danger across seasons. Socks and shoes will avoid the puddles. Deer, bobcats, raccoons, foxes, all tucked away in National parks. That's okay. There's already snow at low altitudes.

They gathered for a feast. Bill had just returned from the war. Shell-schocked in Iraq, he couldn't hold his wine. They tried to draw his attention to the hills that looked like deer skin. He had lost his responses to place. The hullabaloo went on but for a person who wouldn't be there.

The flag is already furled. The late afternoon shadow is spreading. There's no use waiting for the ocean's pronouncements.

3

What is light, waves or numbers? A neighbor leaves his lights lit all night and we know that he's sleepless, or terrified. We paddle in darkness. Vertical skies are sucking up oceans and boats. Tin cities hang on their rocks. Who's scared of invisibility? a blind owl, probably, that old friend, bringer of new worlds.

We're told gods have departed, but who can trust poets? They envision details and bring them to epic dimensions. Being owes them its being. They are its intermediaries, its neurotic go-betweens. Winter is their friend because they freeze together. Together they unclutter views, roads, orchards… Savannah Bay does exist outside the theater; under waves.

Language is sound. To speak is to make modulation, rhythm and tone. An oak tree, under the wind, doesn't speak apple-tree. The light this morning was falling in parallel lines to the redwoods. When is the salmon's season of return? In the air's clarity, the leaf's defining shape, the next town's thunder, where seconds do not crumble, Time shows its aggression. To walk in order to warm up, to think while walking in order to go where one has never been.

There's a species, outside this gravitational field, that, in days of utmost clarity, is aware of us. A tree's rise carries the blood upward. But is the union with that ancient elm truly forbidden? Angels make sounds similar to fading electric instruments. There are holes in space in which airplanes disappear.

Winds murmur into whales' ears rotten leaves' existence. Not too far from their swamp cattle listen to long lines of cars. The air, through a canopy of denuded branches looks chalk-white. Footprints mix with lighter traces of animal paws. Berries are too red for the season; they play games.

Cafés are my homes. One leaves them, carefree, like a child. For the poor, winter is natural habitat: with pockets empty, depleted, belly empty, in an abandoned garden between high-rises, the weather is their enemy although their sole possession. A distant runner within a closed circuit, poverty can't buy heat. Light flows with beatitude in the brain, on the steppes, covers Iraq as well as affluent countries. In decomposing bodies fermentation oozes a perceptible sound. Snow doesn't slow down the process. Anyway, snow doesn't exist everywhere.

Does Bob Grenier think that Cézanne's apple doesn't know it's being looked at? It does, and philosophy's aim is to find out why. If we replaced "Being" with "apple", we'll have favorable long winter nights: apple will shine in the dark and Being will appear like apple's bride.

At certain hours the Garden stands alone. My attention runs along the edges of its octagonal fountain. We live in many places, experience different telluric spirits. At the end, we'll live in all these various places simultaneously. The end.

Winter is a construct. Whose? The mind's? How? A woman exits from the Night Palace and freezes. For a while. Dammit! she yells. Moon hides. Raccoons huddle. The Point revels in thick fog. Foghorn, foghorn. Visibility is nil on the road to North Beach. Same for South Beach.

A few hundred miles north, a matterhorn. Totally covered with fresh snow. Frozen river at its foot. Nothing runs, or breathes. Everything is at a standstill, like it was eons ago.

The season is declining over shallow waters unruffled by the wharf. Mobile distances are not measurable. White lines float with waves, fish and wind. The light pursues them and creates new ones. On the way back the road is straight. Long and thin eucalyptus leaves exude a smell that goes up the head into archaic caverns. That place is as peaceful as the horizon was a few hours ago.

Hale-Bopp came to impregnate our nerve endings. It stopped there. We had gaslights in the mountain house. LUX was the brand name. Immense shadows were spilling outside. Regularly.

Why do some mornings work like narcotics in a young girl's veins? There's no fixed point in the universe; nor in this alley. Life has been tough on the frontline and dull on the backseat. Tonight, full moon behind the clouds.

My thinking is slightly overcast, and traveling. Forests after forests. The woman says: "the young buck is going after the doe." And then she says "rain can't be owned." An Indian is chasing either his own shadow, or a deer's. Rhythms become rimes – out there, on lagoons, mesas, points and ponds, beaches and straits, all obsessed with water.

Revelation did not happen on the mountain but was the mountain, and the fire. In other languages, other things happen. How strange! The universe is at my door. It's entering the room. It's here. It's leaking out.

One sees dead leaves in people's eyes. Terror stricken forces roam over America. This dawn, the sun appeared a few minutes earlier than yesterday.

Bridges in A minor. The eye has appeared so that mind and body do not remain fused. 'Ecriture' is a voyage, travel lines are a writing. The year is not yet over but a young cherry tree has already flowered. Insects will open shop on the poles; pretty soon. It is impossible to think of death because we're faced not with an entity but the end of an activity.

Terror lives in water tables under Earth's crust. Geysers are sprouts of anger as well as of torrid waters. Moby-Dick used to spit fire and water. It got its enemy. Let's celebrate that victory before we sink when our turn arrives. It's very cold outside. The trees are shivering. Instead of bringing blankets to them, Nature denudes them.

But Nature helps to become human. Long shadows descend on the body and reach the heart like they descend on mountains. On a deathbed, the human spirit can cover the whole of the universe. It can figure out Being's auto-creation, its independence from its manifestations, its perpetual death-and-resurrection, experienced as a meteor. Then Nature swells and expands.

We will disappear into that which cannot be named. Language stops at that void. The snow is burned by its own whiteness. The sun rests at its contact. Language waits in the brain, where it's warm; it warms itself up and exits in word patterns. It is in fact a system of sounds borrowed from our instinct for survival. It replaces the deficiencies of our senses and makes up for such things as our lack of fur or of quick reflexes. Space is non-audible sound.

A silver box on a table was considered one's Greek temple. To reach the Veil's other side one needs to already be there. Obviously. Winter is mystic season: a time for the transmutation of the cold into intimacy; of terror, into certitude. Old Tolstoy, where are you, you who knew departure on trains as liberation?

There's agitation in brains, random movements. Ants can lose their minds as often as admirals. Right now, through the window, snow is falling.

Water runs through gutters when it rains. There are networks within plants as well as between them; from vein to vein, from cell to cell, too. First day of the year. In whose calendar? Shake the

47

winter off your mind. Be nothingness. Rest in there. Would years have existed if numbers were not invented? Seasons would have, because of trees. Rains soothe, they drain the fat around the brain.

Air is pushing a voice in my head. It's disturbing. Like childhood did, winter will quit us. Listening to the rain's plock plock on the raincoat was my music. It beat them all. Perception makes the Amazon flow through mythical Babylon. There are seasons that we ignore.

Death is lack of sound. You can pound on it, with fists, with your head. From its side, no answer will come. The dead can see but not hear. Euridyce never heard Orpheus. That's why she didn't come. She wasn't there. No sounds in Hades. Winter: season for loneliness, which is silence.

The moon, tonight, full. I have loved it as if she were a disappeared woman. Uselessly. She's shining. Thank God, not talking!

Perception has to stay alert lest the sunset downs in grayness. Temperatures are dull. Why does the body take so much time to die? On the TV, a she-camel is sobbing; in Mongolia. Nobody else looks unhappy. It's spring on that screen, not in the room. The impossibility of swimming in clear, icy water, is like a curtain drawn across the courtyard. Everywhere, messy sidewalks.

One has to construct oneself in order to believe that one exists. Point Reyes's oaks make the effort. She-camel still sobbing. Bells, at noon, mean funerals. It's reasonable to die in winter. Nowadays History walks like a defeated general whose horses have fallen. (like the trees). They hung Saddam Hussein and went fucking. It never snows in Baghdad.

It's hard to distinguish memory from imagination. To produce a lily required surprising strategies. Was the angel of the Annunciation as husky as a long-distance flying airman? The new writing is not a stream – it dried out with global warming, but a wakeful dreaming.

Time tipped over from my hands. Then it rained a green oil.

Streets started to crack. No sun is boiling over the earth. One can't foresee any uninterrupted bliss for matter's creatures. We're sound waves. Prometheus is unbound and bewildered. A free fall for him.

History presents us a new method for looking at it as if a spherical, though open continuum. The world's presence in the mind defines the mind, which can also mirror the world. The mirror is often obscure. What they call Being plays tricks to itself. It produces the world and leaves it, receding into itself by the same action.

Paper-crowns. Cylinders made from vegetal materials. Blackish columns filled with sap. Traces of pools. Reminders of green bark. Metal chairs. Empty and fenced sandy backyards. Gone travelers. Fountains shut off. Marble stairs. Ceramic pots resting on balustrades. Low gray sky with sunken clouds. Early nightfall. Extinct streetlights. Ice formations.

Light helps the day rise from its wreckage. After much commotion, it withdraws. The danger of befriending it is that it is treacherous. The ocean is there, wide open. There's air and love together. Bodies meander in the dark guided by an inner compass. Leaves have fallen, have rotten. Ancient stories are retold.

Strange thoughts are produced by the weather and like plants thrive on fresh water. Sometimes, they sink in abysses of ice. They can melt, catch fire or die of thirst. On the river Elbe's frozen surface Friedrich N. abandoned his thinking powers and let himself lie headless, bleeding, silenced. On the way to the beatific vision, he was probably arrested. Danger is familiar territory.

To relish the winter when under duress, to look at white bears frolicking on ice, envy shamelessly their joy, what an achievement! To be, oh to be! When the imagination lands you on its fastest horse back into your walled city, you know that you have shed the best of you.

Writing puts the world on hold. When the ceremony is over, the light appears to have changed abruptly. We are sensors, and make the mistake of thinking that we are in control

The self is in a perpetual representation of itself. *Ecce Homo.* Death is the interruption of a monstrosity. Animals stay out of the consciousness of their transience and that leads them to a particular kind of melancholy. This century doesn't seem to offer much room for thoughts that are private.

The river is a luxury within the city; its artery and its soul. Plane and chestnut trees reign over the night while a feeling of estrangement seizes the inhabitants. Bridges cease to be mysterious but are still magnificent.

What is this place we call sky, that recedes when we fly the way the horizon does when we sail?! To see is to think.

Clarity is single, and it's the wind's opposite. The spirit soars. Its center is to be found everywhere. Some passersby take street lamps for overblown flowers. The river flows as if it were a train station with all trains recently gone. Many shores have been created for an ocean.

The homeless have faces carved by the temperatures. O dark side of the moon, oh to be there! Wingless birds are space-blind, but the ocean is altogether a luminous eye. The mind could be crammed with information but a drop of blood can silence it indefinitely.

The salt spread on the moon makes it shine. No heat for the bones. Sheets of water on the march scare the hills. A shadow precedes the intellect and that's why the latter springs from a zone of total obscurity that's sometimes mistakenly named nothingness.

Clouds have to prove their existence. Airplanes fly through but do not allow anyone to open a window and touch them. Summer clouds are different from the winter ones. Our minds are porous to clouds, made probably from the same stuff. Although it's not necessary to sleep in order to remember, it's necessary to remember in order to be.

The hottest lands in Africa decimate vegetal life. It's not the land, it's the sun, double star, giver and killer. They decimate animal thinking too. The sky is often an implacable enemy, another God.

To pull in the shutters, light a fire, let one's mental functions follow their ways, and stumble on the notion of irrational numbers. To displace the irrational to where its opposite resides. Then, suddenly, the separation between sea and sky becomes a point of departure. That ambiguity surpasses the mystery of numbers, but why?

Today, the squirrels of the park couldn't bundle up. It was snowing. The moon, says Joanne K., is the gate to heaven. Tonight, the super-casino is closed because it's canceled out by the weather. The sea is so wild that nothing will ever bring her back to sanity.

Eyeglasses do not help us see the eucalyptus grow but in dreams those rise instantly from a ferruginous soil. What's here to be looked at? a row of inkpots, the air's pollution, vibrations left by a phone-call; and, when eyes are closed, a fiery curtain.

Why do we love the invisible when we can never hold it in our hands? We probably like the word more than the object. Thoughts start underground and bring from there some mud to the brain. With slush on the boots we think of clouded transparencies.

Being a creature of the weather I'm fused with it. Air is my ocean, and the ocean is mine. Miles of frozen orchards punctuate the emptiness. They breathe, though with difficulty. Numbers were created in their proximity, as well as theories of serial happenings. Air drafts push through them their irrational journeys.

Why did we invent sky deities? Minds are little batteries. Some of those take a person to work and bring him back, that's all. Bigger ones are industrial plants: they carry a crew of astronauts to the moon. Once in a very great while they take you to the inception of the Big Bang.

Can I claim Homer for ancestry? Pure thinking doesn't mention proper names, but the hell with it. Am looking for the perfect wave.

The forest: its fragrance, its thickness, its power to blind. Would this particular oak be cut, and logged to make fires, the kind that children watch as an encounter with magic? It will burn like soldiers in Iraq, sailors in Salamina. What is it "to burn"? Are flames, in their intimacy more radical than water?

Trees have many lives thanks to their yearly encounter with the spring. They sink into the ground, where animals don't, their souls being lighter, closer to the ignored origin. They know whoever is coming and that to be is to revolve around chaos.

When a full forest burns winter is puzzled. No hell in civilizations' writings has any acquaintance with the splendor of planetary fires. Life's beginning – if a beginning there was – must have been an overheated particle of light.

Oh please! Nature is no metaphor, but the origin of itself, and of its manifestations, and that includes language which is produced in order to give it a name.

Like a paperweight the sky, though imprecise, weighs on the body. It's a cannibalistic situation. Creatures eat and are eaten. Night is felt not as an immense land but as a wall. Still, space remains open.

Valleys carved out of granite are visited by waterfalls that turn them into a paradise that convinces us of the necessity to be born. In the winter those falls hibernate but we remember.

A universal law wants water to freeze, prescribes sleep to exhausted bodies, finds soul mates for the lonely, closes bars at the early hours of the sunrise.

The weather keeps us conscious of our existence. The skin mediates fate. To be water in water, snow meeting rain, diffused, drifting, breaking down in moisture or smoke, diluting into near nothingness, that's the mind's destination. Drops of dew on a morning rose have as much being as a stack of accumulated thoughts.

A river is running down this property. For a free trip to the moon, the human species is waiting in line, and so is the river.

4

    A tempest of heat. The brain's evaporation is a possibility. Taxicabs are refusing to put on the air-conditioner so they let the car be a furnace. One's body seems destined to be roasted but the brain is used to keep its own temperature. How can such a gelatinous organ conceive the most lethal weapons that the military produces?

    Life originates in moisture, slippery bellies, opaque liquids. It dries up, we must convene. A sea-elephant gives birth to a barking pup. Vultures pick up not yet totally born creatures in their beaks. Birth and death imply heat and blood. Animals are getting insane for lack of water. No one is here. Pure blue color, all the way.

The weather takes us in its stride. The promise is not the rain, is the water. Trees move in spherical directions while we wither away. They burst with leaves higher than one's vision. A heat wave is spreading.

The sea is boiling, opening its belly. Revelation needs heat; brains that evaporate steaming thoughts. Then the mirage becomes reality. In agony, the light. In poverty, the future's birth. Then again the curse against war machines uttered by the sun. But the sun is ever exploding death into life.

Behind the trembling moisture there are desperate faces and bodies still alive under gunfire. Is weather temperature, is it definable, is it not oceanic, and metaphysical? Shadows last longer when they follow summer days and bring lovers together.

Heat: young girls smelling sperm, fish slowing their swim, birds sleeping under large banana leaves. Weather, more democratic than governments, to say the least. The sea, implacable mirror, forbidden. The woman exits from the Night Palace, walks straight, never looking back.

The mind sizzles as a vaporous intermediary between matter and spirit. Summer and spirit melt into each other. Sexuality works in similar ways. Shadows get to be merciful, like a hedge of wild berries calming down the redwing blackbirds.

One step at a time, uphill, closer to the sky: the heart is in danger, one faints or suffers a stroke. In the Peloponnesus one understands how Medea killed Jason's sons, who were her own. And that woman, burning with beauty, crosses over the sea. The mist blinds her view. How can one think through the air's thickness?

The mountains are quietly waiting. Dry soil. Broken cars. The cold is forgotten. On that sheet of burning metal that the sea has become passengers are suffocating. Water and ideas disappeared on the moon.

Soldiers sent to the war have their clothes melting into their skin. It's a season for delirium. To conquer Iraq is to defy hell. One's moral fiber can turn into spiritual mush. Reptiles keep hidden.

Summer clouds are suddenly friendly, sailing low. Keepers of memory. The brain presses on the eyes, on one's breath, creating for the body new rhythmic patterns. Separated from the will, thinking becomes a widower, a late season moon. No matter what, trees will refuse to die of thirst, of heat.

Divinities, knights, mounted cavalries, all gone.

Arthur Bierman raises a brain storm over a single subject: "the square of opposition." Philosophers of his kind are meta-poets. Their illuminations do not descend on other heads but dissipate in surrounding air. Deport reason!

The sky is porcelain blue. An egg boils instantly when covered with burning sand. Better wait for the clouds' return. The ocean is licking its borders. Light is breathing.

What's meant by 'Being'?

How crowded are the days under Tammuz's rule! A bull, a woman, a man, any would do in days of frenzy. The sun oozed out of its circle and filled the sky. Underneath, everything turned into a sign.

Alchemy enters the mind at night and creates unsustainable reverberations. Drunk is one's summer dream, like the "Vita Nuova" plunged in anticipation, constant reenactment of the distraction of the self by the self.

Noon divides the day into competing parts whose reunification is perfect impossibility. Not a leaf has stirred. All the constellations are up there, hidden by a single star's power.

A bird managed to fly; it landed on a burning roof. One wing exhaled smoke. There's no way for one's spirit to navigate over stilled waters. The human principle is active in bodies exposed to sunrays even when the mind has left and is hovering above the ocean.

All Mediterranean harbors are lampposts. Madras is sweltering under a lunatic moon. Summer gives eminence to cities.

How small the world compared to a mind! But isn't the universe a mega-brain? How to know? By intuition, by kinship? Well, forget your question, call it quits, call it death.

A cup of tea contains grace. In a late afternoon, nothing moves, save one's heart. Let time go by in its undisturbed journey. The woman is out of the Night Palace. She turned off the lights. Today she's alone in her garden. Not alone but surrounded with fruit trees that gave their full. Resting. She thinks of rebirth without the need for dying. Life is always, (she says, – and writes) the coming wave.

By the Sacramento Delta the weather triumphs over the will. Sailing straight into the heat, vision becomes slim and focused. With all dark angels having taken refuge in hotel rooms, people wander around lagoons, canals…

A line of fluid blue is just there. I am this sun and it is me. A dilatation of the senses. Brick walls and closed windows. A brain jammed with video images. Flies feeding on an ice-cream cone. The big mess of having a life.

A summer night's music. We're inserted in that history. A translation of the world in sounds mixed with silence. Walls supporting emptiness. Trees can enter if they want. Sounds muffled. Beds, soft.

Has anybody studied the geometry of clouds? They're continents on the move. Boats are cutting through near-immaterial waves. It's with their shadows that one can deal, shadows that have ways to disappear.

Flowers, in their pots, are happy to be on windowsills. All around, the ground is dry and warm. All around, the place is gently empty.

Representation is collaboration between mind and world. This passing cloud is mine and it is yours, but not ours. The mind is in love with the world.

Hills grow apart and come together. The mountain functions on different wavelengths. It rained recently. Thunder swept the heavy sky. It rained again. There's fear of destruction. All traffic is disrupted because of floods. Small towns are covered by the night. It's agreeable to feel cool in the midst of this summer's heat while the world is boiling over with anger.

Westward the wind blows with all manners of difficulty. The earth is shaking at its boundaries. The journey to the sea remains fearsome. These vacations do not assure rest, to say the least. In spite of disasters one's spirit will fight for water, and the elusive need to think.

To go to the wilderness in order to give names to certain things: word is power. Are the mountain slopes climbing or descending? In their crevasses, stones stir. Once in a while one of them rolls, finds a new ground. Life bursts from every corner; why then there's no place where people won't die?

The only absolute this mind can apprehend is the pleasure of being only a temporary visitor to this transient garden. That happened ten minutes ago. A summer breeze is worth a night of love.

Color is a variety of light. Beyond the lake, what else besides the remembrance of it as a shimmering mist over a spread of water? It's good to then cross arid territory with an empty mind.

It's a day where the light is gone, the night too. A day in the past, when officers of the Red Army went to war, and the day when Hamlet disappeared in fog, never to be seen again. The brain thinks in a total darkness. For the heart, things are different. It bleeds on a soil which is far away. That sacrificial ground has a name: Iraq, this thing that merchants of death have transformed into killing fields.

Nowadays fire is eating up the country that stole it first from the gods. Cremation. Chaotic pain. Lungs drying up in both the workers of evil and their preys. Thus, reality breaks down, unfounded.

O light infallible! Born from lit chaos. The heat has lifted. Iridescent clouds are openly challenging the sky. A patch of sunlight rests on the roof next to a mass of grayish hues.

Trumpets are blowing for a parade of souls proclaiming their maddening will to live. The light descends on its own pace to signal the day's end. But the night is more potent. It's feverish. It opens up other doors. What city is this? It has a river, and trees that keep growing in the dark.

An angel is sweeping the air with its wings. It says that waiting for voices can be dangerous. Tiring, for sure. Pick up the baggage and leave. Just leave. Don't bother with rainbows.

To write and to know that one is writing, and that it takes time, and decision, and ink, and, simultaneously, see that there's a ceiling above, a chair, a rug, that there's breathing while writing, and an inhaling of warm, insalubrious air, and a wave visiting like grace, like paper; and there are little signs called letters, bigger ones called words, and thoughts under the guise of lines…

There's anger in the air. A time for solar storms, disoriented comets, volcanic eruptions within black holes; for driftwood in the background, ducks on slime. Imagination is flaring up, reappropriating its copper. The sun, copper tray, tribal chief with planets chained to its destiny.

Confusion, being contagious, is affecting the park. Streaks of the coming autumn are touching the branches. Political uncertainty has reached the vegetal world, which can hardly deal with its own upheaval. Some trees thrive under the weather's harshness while others succumb.

Desire broke loose this morning, with hunger in the stomach, insomnia on the mind. Which of the past or the future has more reality? What of the murderous sun that's obliterating the sky and being too strong for making shadows?

From within a Shakespearian drama how does the world look? A curve, a forest, chambless. Streams of words are exchanged while solitude grows, dragging the self into evanescence.

An ominous thunder. The weather is bringing the Tropics to Europe. The moon is asked to add one more summer to this one. It's hard to see beyond.

To return with the morning paper mediating inconceivable news. There was a universe which contracted to the infinitesimal point of the Big Bang, and then expansion picked up steam again.

Memories follow each other like prayer beads and rivers run as easily as thoughts of the monsoon. At this very moment birds fly very high; how do they view these humans crowding the streets?

It's cooler in the tombs than outside. Outside begins the furnace where armies melt. There are other things than the weather, but these days they are hard to find. The sky is empowered by the sun's stubborness.

A trace is sometimes persistent, a scratch on the retina, a mark on the brain. The heat has gathered dust on the windows. We gasp for light. We're not unpredictable.

  A deep darkness intervenes and makes cracks in one's reasoning. Not to fall. Not to forget. Indications of a chaotic heart. In a haggard palace, the woman drifts. Heads of emperors are placed at some strategic points with the intention of bringing fear to her soul. She doesn't respond. The sea, wide open, roars in her brain, brain and sea fused.

  If there's not a forest, there's a hill. Drinking and bathing are small animals' favorite games. Trains are running late. Traffic jams in one's brain emit strange sounds. To dance at that tune. Lightning precedes a summer storm. Does burn the body and the land.

  Dionysus visited Sikyonou. They made him (like me) an honorary citizen. He climbed on the stage and from his throat went a cry. Ever since plays are performed all over during summers, in the heat, the discomfort, after long rides and sleepless nights. Any play is the staging of a resurrection. Seasonal resurrections.

People come and settle on a given piece of earth. They legitimate their action by acting it on a stage. Oedipus blinds himself in public under a merciless hour. The founding scene of Tragedy will be repeated through time.

Beware says Dionysus, I preceded you in this marriage of wine and fame and it ended in the dislocation of my body and my soul. Hot winds blew when the Barbarian women drank his blood. But the latter, still, tasted better than uranium; mushrooms didn't look like brains, then.

A paper fan, with one blow, killed a wasp. The animal's companion made a tour of the garden and came back near the little corpse. It lay its legs on it, pushed it to the table's edge, and took it down with him. In the meantime, Greece is burning.

The lilacs are breathing heavily. The fig tree's leaves are making patterns against the wall. In a purely material universe would God keep his usefulness? The world is fated to pursue the search for its own self.

People die on a certain spot and the rain continues to fall. We return to the Night Palace where our loneliness responds to the solitude of the elements. Transfiguration creates emptiness around itself. Probably because of its nocturnal quality, the Palace exudes uncertainty about its own existence.

Is Nature's folly a response to ours? There's cataclysm in the air, something like a scene of cockroaches running in panic. Not to water gardens with the Pacific's help.

Above the horizon the pink is immaterial, and below, ethereal. I have taken some sunrises for sunsets.

It's a time for the trees, their fertility. Uranus and Earth, through rain and thunder, a marriage. A goat, running wild, has luminous eyes. His skin, the color of the land. Being is either silent or inaudible. Speedboats bring medusas to the harbor.

Are the pipelines of blood running in the bodies of the Arabs less worthy than the oil running under their grounds? What's History's worth? The Grand Canyon runs a river of fire.

   Heat erases intelligence when memory is already gone. Then a heap of flesh and bones looks inconsequential. There have been nights of music and luxury. A woman came here, lay down on the grass, in the penumbra, little noticed.

   The roar is not coming from the ocean but from the world. Is the atom bomb humanism's logical end or its counterpart, a balancing act for the restoration of death's dominion?

   Seasonal thoughts are unsystematic. Mineral reality states its pride. The sunlight's triumph gives us a taste of eternity. Flies and bees go insane on violence. A pebble. A grain of sand. A rusted nail. A murmur from a human being begging for coolness. Gods are jealous of human mortality.

   And a question: do angels cross seas? An archaic wind gathers vigor, sweeps the land and tempts the imagination which is trying to find the secret passage from one season to the next.

The sun aligns itself with the sea to batter the shores. Thyme and sage distribute their scent through a friendly forest. Scent is language as much as a perspiration. Signs of life are gradually reduced to essentials and in the process the steady rhythm of a noticeable tide reaches an hallucinatory grandeur.

Women are keepers of their own story, therefore they're historians. Looking without thinking is pure knowledge, fusion, the only way to see that between the fig tree and the geranium bush lies space's mystery.

Disappearance is reverse apparition. Counter action from the tip of the scale, Moby-Dick on one plate, Ahab on the other. What happened after their death?

In some places, the uninterrupted presence of the gods is part of the environment. Fires return. We learn our politics from the weather that imprisons, unifies, kills or spares. Here, insurgency is written on the sun's face. Civilizations are as bankrupt as the banks. The dream factory disappeared with Baghdad's Library.

Now that matter has been made immaterial, is man going to be made un-human?

Evenings are sliding, going nowhere. Trees are capable of passion. The apricot and the mulberry don't lose sight of each other; they travel in pair and utter inspired and ancient sounds when they mate, tearing the night apart, not unlike lightning.

Whistling in the staircase a young man, wind on his side, is entering the Night Palace, where Being is all upside-down. A fish on a plate. A lander is sent to Mars. What would the temperatures do to the landed instruments? Would the planet have from there on a destiny?

As a concept, the season has died. Its reality escapes us. It deals probably with other realities at whose doors we stand, puzzled, although we're completely engaged with them. To swim in the ocean's salt is medicine for all kinds of wounds, of questions.

 There's a weather report from Brooklyn: life is pleasant by the harbor. Liners have proliferated but there's plenty of maritime space left. A multitude of signs are raining. Two pomegranates on the windowsill make the day blissful.

 Where has Earth been during this long night? Where are the river, the bridge, the land? At which point are we alone? Did Virginia Woolf commit suicide because Perceval didn't return from India?

 Are we a dream, a nightmare, a fulfillment? The desire for permanence has given way to the eminence of the ephemeral. That's why air drafts, dance, cinema or fire are privileged; they disappear as they come. To be is a process that we're searching for while it's already here. We are the looking, the heat, and the voyage.